Birds in the Air

Eleanor Burns

For Brian — my companion birdwatcher!

First printing August, 2001

Published by Quilt in a Day®, Inc.
1955 Diamond St, San Marcos, CA 92069

ISBN 1-891776-07-X

Art Director Merritt Voigtlander

Contents

Introduction

The Birds in the Air quilt is symbolic of flight or migration. During the Underground Railroad in the 1840's to 1850's, a clever quilter could indicate a direction for fugitives to travel through the choice of fabric and placement of blocks. In the cover quilt, notice the blocks in one area are light, creating an arrow pointing North.

A Birds in the Air directional quilt was originally designed by Deborah Coates, wife of Quaker Lindley Coates, of Lancaster County, Pennsylvania. They were abolitionists, and ran Safe House #5 on the Underground Railroad.

According to oral family history, two granddaughters of Deborah could not agree on who should inherit the precious quilt. So, with the Quaker sense of equality, it was decided to cut the quilt exactly in half. When the raw edges were bound over, a small central image of a bound slave was almost totally obscured. Underneath the image were these words: "Deliver me from the oppression of man." When the quilt was passed on to a single descendant, the bindings were opened and the image was brought together again.

That quilt was just one family's way of helping emancipate the slaves!

Construction of eight blocks takes 1½ hours, which is perfect for a busy schedule. Fly free while you try this easy method.

Eleanor Burns

About the Quilt

The Birds in the Air block finishes at approximately 6" square. It is divided into three distinct parts.

In this example:

> **Background** is the light pieces.
> **Birds** are the three small dark triangles.
> **Nest** is the matching large triangle.

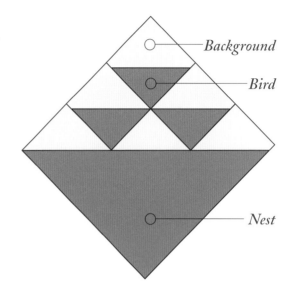

Choose from these fabric selections:

> Two Fabrics

> One Background with
> Multi-Fabric Nests and Birds

> Multi-Fabric Background and
> Multi-Fabric Nests and Birds

It is best if you select 100% cotton fabrics from the same fabric line. Yardage charts are based on using fabrics at least 40" wide.

On Point Settings

The On Point Setting is the first of two settings, with blocks assembled on point in diagonal rows with Background triangles at the edges. Simple Borders or Sawtooth Borders are added around the outside edges.

Two Fabrics

Eleanor Burns   *Wallhanging 37" x 37"*

One Background and Multi-Fabric Nests and Birds

Sue Bouchard   *Wallhanging 37" x 37"*

Eleanor Burns chose a peaceful blue Nests and Birds fabric, and set them off with a stark Background in off-white tone on tone. The thirteen blocks set on point make a traditional or contemporary statement, depending on the surroundings. The Background is repeated in the First and Third Borders, showing off the Two Direction Sawtooth Border. The Blue Birds of Happiness are from Eleanor's line of fabrics, Rainbow Florals.

Sue Bouchard selected a stunning black Background to set off her thirteen blocks of colorful Birds. The seven charming small scale prints used for the Nests and Birds are from Eleanor's line of fabric named Rainbow Florals manufactured by Benartex. Surrounding these cheerful Nightingales singing in the night is a bright garden stripe!

Multi-Fabric Background and
Multi-Fabric Nests and Birds

Teresa Varnes   *Lap Robe 42" x 58"*

Teresa Varnes created festive holiday Birds in the Air blocks, and set them together on point. Beige Backgrounds accented with large red roses and climbing vines are combined with cardinal reds and parrot greens in varying scales of prints. Mirthful Side Triangles cut from 10½" squares capture the holiday Birds. For an old-fashioned look, Teresa chose not to add Borders, and finished with a bright red Binding.

Straight Settings

The second setting is a straight setting, with all blocks turned in the same direction, or turned as blades in a pinwheel. The quilt is finished with a Simple Border, or a Sawtooth Border.

Two Fabrics

Loretta Smith   *Queen 84" x 102"*

Loretta Smith created this striking quilt, straight setting blocks together in the pinwheel design. The strong graphic design sets those blades into motion! The two fabrics, a small scale Background and large scale Birds and Nest, contrast in color and value, with the darker fabric setting the tone for the quilt. Birds flying straight in one direction are captured in the Sawtooth Border!

One Background and Multi-Fabric Nests and Birds

Multi-Fabric Background and Multi-Fabric Nests and Birds

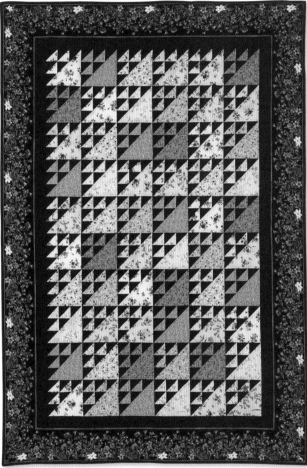

Teresa Varnes   *Twin 50" x 74"*

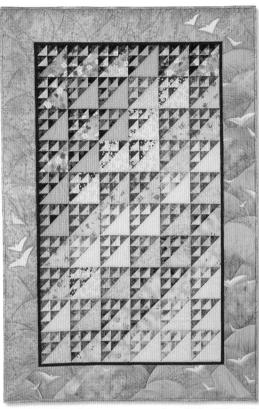

Patricia Knoechel   *Lap Robe 50" x 74"*

Teresa Varnes sewed sunny bright Birds with one saturated black Background fabric, and placed them together in a straight setting. Happy as larks, eight different sets of Birds perch upon their matching Nests. The First Border, same as the Background, encloses the Birds, and a 7" Second Border floral stripe keeps them chirping in the garden. All the vibrant fabrics are from the Rainbow Floral line by Eleanor Burns for Benartex.

Patricia Knoechel was inspired by her Oriental fabric collection for her contemporary Birds in the Air quilt. Aptly named Border Crossing, appliqued Birds fly freely over the blocks into the left border and blue yonder. Eight different Nests and Birds in light to medium fabrics are arranged in graduating order. The same number of Backgrounds, also in graduating order, soar with the Birds! A striking 1" Border and 7" Borders in contrasting fabrics on two opposite sides complete the flight.

9

Two Block Patches

Traditionally, Birds in the Air blocks were made from triangles with bias edges. Stretch from the bias made piecing perfect blocks difficult. In this unique Quilt in a Day method, individual triangles and bias edges are eliminated. This is a brief overview of the Birds in the Air technique.

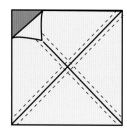

Make Birds by layering 6" squares of Background and Bird fabrics.

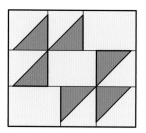

Make Two Block Patches with six Birds and three rectangles.

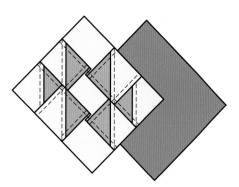

Pair Birds with oversized Nests cut at 7" x 8".

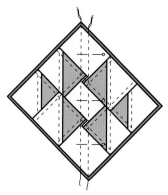

Draw lines and sew on lines.

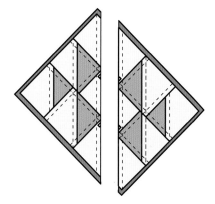

Cut Two Block Patch in half.

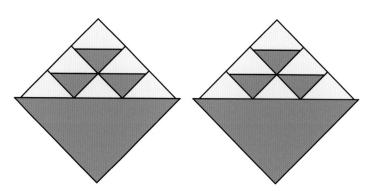

Like magic, two Birds in the Air blocks result!

Two Fabric Quilts

In this Wallhanging, Sue Bouchard made two sets of four Two Block Patches for a total of sixteen blocks. Three were extra! She set them together on point with a Two Direction Sawtooth Border. The First Border is Background fabric, and the Third Border is Nests and Birds fabric.

Two sets of eight identical blocks

Multi-Fabric Quilts

In this Lap Robe, Lori Forsythe used one Background with eight different Nests and Birds fabrics. She made eight different sets of Two Block Patches for a total of 64 blocks. She only needed 59, so was happy to eliminate some of her not-so-perfect blocks!

Eight sets of eight identical blocks

Multi-Fabric Wallhanging

For variety, Multi-Fabric Wallhanging instructions show how to make only one Two Block Patch from each pair of fabrics. Since this is unique, specific instructions appear in blue, referring to Multi-Fabric Wallhangings with one Background or Multi-Fabric Backgrounds (columns 2 and 3 on pages 14 and 15).

Teresa Varnes made seven Two Block Patches and cut them in half, for a total of fourteen. She chose to place the brightest block in the center, and eliminated the second identical one. Two Birds left over from each set were used in the Sawtooth Border.

Seven sets of two identical blocks

Supplies

Two of the most useful rulers for making Birds in the Air blocks quickly are the 6½" Triangle Square Up and 12" Quick Quarter .

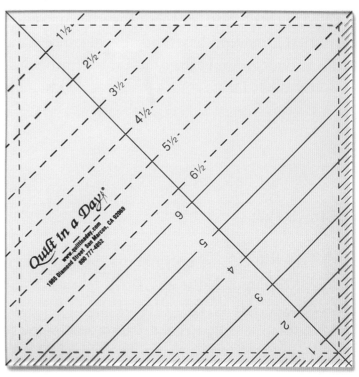

6½" Triangle Square Up Ruler
from Quilt in a Day

Use the Triangle Square Up ruler for squaring up 2½" pieced squares up to 6½" Bird blocks. See pages 30 and 49 for instructions.

QR-QQ2 Ruler

12" Quick Quarter
from Quilter's Rule International

Use the Quick Quarter for marking lines ½" apart on the Bird blocks. It's a light weight turquoise ruler 12" long and ½" wide with a slot down the center. See page 45 for instructions.

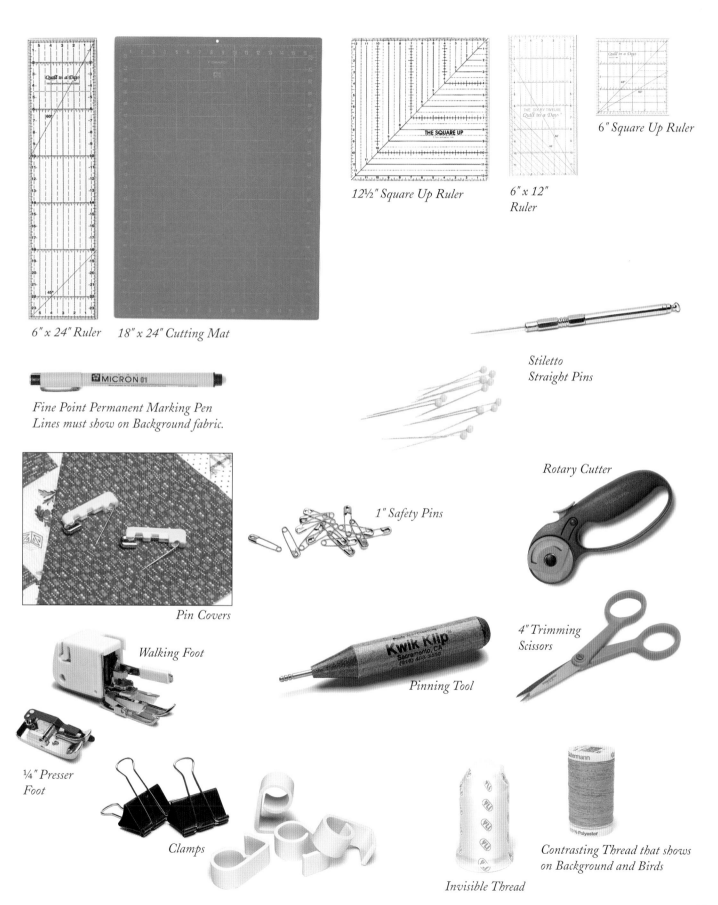

6" x 24" Ruler

18" x 24" Cutting Mat

12½" Square Up Ruler

6" x 12" Ruler

6" Square Up Ruler

Stiletto

Straight Pins

Fine Point Permanent Marking Pen Lines must show on Background fabric.

Rotary Cutter

Pin Covers

1" Safety Pins

4" Trimming Scissors

Walking Foot

Pinning Tool

¼" Presser Foot

Clamps

Invisible Thread

Contrasting Thread that shows on Background and Birds

Wallhanging

	Two Fabrics	One Background Multi-Fabric Nests and Birds	Multi-Fabric Background, Nests and Birds

Background	½ yd
	(1) 6" strip cut into
	   (6) 6" squares
	(2) 2½" strips cut into
	   (24) 2½" x 3¼"
		⅔ yd
		(2) 6" strips cut into
		   (7) 6" squares
		(2) 2 ½" strips cut into
		   (21) 2½" x 3¼"
			7 Different ¼ yds
			from each cut
			(1) 6" square
			(3) 2½" x 3¼"

Nests and Birds
   Nests
 	
   Birds
	⅔ yd
	(2) 7" strips cut into
	   (8) 7" x 8"
	(1) 6" strip cut into
	   (6) 6" squares
		7 Different ¼ yds
		from each cut
		(1) 7" x 8"
		
		(1) 6" square
			7 Different ¼ yds
			from each cut
			(1) 7" x 8"
			
			(1) 6" square

Edge Triangles	⅓ yd (2) 10½" squares (2) 6" squares	⅓ yd (2) 10½" squares (2) 6" squares	⅓ yd (2) 10½" squares (2) 6" squares
First Border	⅓ yd (4) 2" strips	⅓ yd (4) 2" strips	⅓ yd (4) 2" strips
Second Border Simple	 ⅓ yd (4) 2½" strips	 ⅓ yd (4) 2½" strips	 ⅓ yd (4) 2½" strips
Or			

Sawtooth
   Background
 	
   Birds
	½ yd
	(2) 6" strips cut into
	   (7) 6" squares
	(4) 2½" squares
	
	½ yd
	(2) 6" strips cut into
	   (7) 6" squares
		½ yd
		(2) 6" strips cut into
		   (7) 6" squares
		(4) 2½" squares
		
		From above ¼ yds
		(7) 6" squares
			From above ¼ yds
			(7) 6" squares
			(4) 2½" squares
			
			From above ¼ yds
			(7) 6" squares

Third Border	½ yd (4) 3" strips	½ yd (4) 3" strips	½ yd (4) 3" strips
Binding	½ yd (4) 3" strips	½ yd (4) 3" strips	½ yd (4) 3" strips
Backing	45" x 45"	45" x 45"	45" x 45"
Batting	45" x 45"	45" x 45"	45" x 45"

Wallhanging

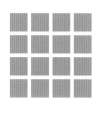

	Two Fabrics	One Background Multi-Fabric Nests and Birds	Multi-Fabric Background, Nests and Birds
Background	½ yd (1) 6" strip cut into (6) 6" squares (2) 2 ½" strips cut into (24) 2½" x 3¼"	⅔ yd (2) 6" strips cut into (8) 6" squares (3) 2 ½" strips cut into (32) 2½" x 3¼"	8 Different ¼ yds from each cut (1) 6" square (3) 2½" x 3¼"
Nests and Birds	⅔ yd	8 Different ¼ yds	8 Different ¼ yds
Nests	(2) 7" strips cut into (8) 7" x 8"	from each cut (1) 7" x 8"	from each cut (1) 7" x 8"
Birds	(1) 6" strip cut into (6) 6" squares	(1) 6" square	(1) 6" square
First Border	⅓ yd (4) 2½" strips	⅓ yd (4) 2½" strips	⅓ yd (4) 2½" strips
Second Border			
Simple	⅓ yd (4) 2½" strips	⅓ yd (4) 2½" strips	⅓ yd (4) 2½" strips
Or			
Sawtooth Background	½ yd (2) 6" strips cut into (7) 6" squares (4) 2½" squares	½ yd (2) 6" strips cut into (7) 6" squares (4) 2½" squares	From above ¼ yds (7) 6" squares (4) 2½" squares
Birds	½ yd (2) 6" strips cut into (7) 6" squares	From above ¼ yds (7) 6" squares	From above ¼ yds (7) 6" squares
Third Border	½ yd (4) 3" strips	½ yd (4) 3" strips	½ yd (4) 3" strips
Binding	½ yd (4) 3" strips	½ yd (4) 3" strips	½ yd (4) 3" strips
Backing	45" x 45"	45" x 45"	45" x 45"
Batting	45" x 45"	45" x 45"	45" x 45"

Lap Robe

	Two Fabrics	One Background Multi-Fabric Nests and Birds	Multi-Fabric Background, Nests and Birds
Background	1½ yds (4) 6" strips cut into 　　(24) 6" squares (8) 2½" strips cut into 　　(96) 2½" x 3¼"	1½ yds (4) 6" strips cut into 　　(24) 6" squares (8) 2½" strips cut into 　　(96) 2½" x 3¼"	8 Different ¼ yds from each cut (3) 6" squares (12) 2½" x 3¼"
Nests and Birds	2¼ yds	8 Different ½ yds	8 Different ½ yds
Nests	(7) 7" strips cut into 　　(32) 7" x 8"	from each cut (4) 7" x 8"	from each cut (4) 7" x 8"
Birds	(4) 6" strips cut into 　　(24) 6" squares	(3) 6" squares	(3) 6" squares
Edge Triangles	¾ yd (5) 10½" squares (2) 6" squares	¾ yd (5) 10½" squares (2) 6" squares	¾ yd (5) 10½" squares (2) 6" squares
First Border	⅔ yd (6) 3" strips	⅔ yd (6) 3" strips	⅔ yd (6) 3" strips
Second Border			
Simple	⅔ yd (7) 2½" strips	⅔ yd (7) 2½" strips	⅔ yd (7) 2½" strips
Or			
Sawtooth Background	⅔ yd (3) 6" strips cut into 　　(14) 6" squares (4) 2½" squares	⅔ yd (3) 6" strips cut into 　　(14) 6" squares (4) 2½" squares	From above ¼ yds (14) 6" squares (4) 2½" squares
Birds	⅔ yd (3) 6" strips cut into 　　(14) 6" squares	From above ½ yds (14) 6" squares	From above ½ yds (14) 6" squares
Third Border	¾ yd (7) 3½" strips	¾ yd (7) 3½" strips	¾ yd (7) 3½" strips
Binding	⅔ yd (7) 3" strips	⅔ yd (7) 3" strips	⅔ yd (7) 3" strips
Backing	64" x 81"	64" x 81"	64" x 81"
Batting	64" x 81"	64" x 81"	64" x 81"

Lap Robe

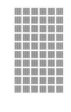

	Two Fabrics	One Background Multi-Fabric Nests and Birds	Multi-Fabric Background, Nests and Birds

Background	1½ yds
	(4) 6" strips cut into
	    (24) 6" squares
	(8) 2½" strips cut into
	    (96) 2½" x 3¼"
		1½ yds
		(4) 6" strips cut into
		    (24) 6" squares
		(8) 2½" strips cut into
		    (96) 2½" x 3¼"
			8 Different ¼ yds
			from each cut
			(3) 6" squares
			(12) 2½" x 3¼"

Nests and Birds
  Nests
 	
  Birds
	2¼ yds
	(7) 7" strips cut into
	    (32) 7" x 8"
	(4) 6" strips cut into
	    (24) 6" squares
		8 Different ½ yds
		from each cut
		(4) 7" x 8"
		(3) 6" squares
			8 Different ½ yds
			from each cut
			(4) 7" x 8"
			(3) 6" squares

First Border	½ yd (6) 2½" strips	½ yd (6) 2½" strips	½ yd (6) 2½" strips
Second Border Simple	½ yd (6) 2½" strips	½ yd (6) 2½" strips	½ yd (6) 2½" strips
Or			

Sawtooth
  Background
	⅔ yd
	(3) 6" strips cut into
	    (13) 6" squares
	(4) 2½" squares
		⅔ yd
		(3) 6" strips cut into
		    (13) 6" squares
		(4) 2½" squares
			From above ¼ yds
			(13) 6" squares
			(4) 2½" squares

Birds	½ yd (2) 6" strips cut into (13) 6" squares	From above ½ yds (13) 6" squares	From above ½ yds (13) 6" squares
Third Border	¾ yd (7) 3½" strips	¾ yd (7) 3½" strips	¾ yd (7) 3½" strips
Binding	¾ yd (7) 3" strips	¾ yd (7) 3" strips	¾ yd (7) 3" strips
Backing	58" x 82"	58" x 82"	58" x 82"
Batting	58" x 82"	58" x 82"	58" x 82"

Twin Quilt

	Two Fabrics	One Background Multi-Fabric Nests & Birds	Multi-Fabric Background, Nest and Birds
Background	1⅔ yds (5) 6" strips cut into 　(30) 6" squares (10) 2½" strips cut into 　(120) 2½" x 3¼"	1⅔ yds (5) 6" strips cut into 　(30) 6" squares (10) 2½" strips cut into 　(120) 2½" x 3¼"	10 Different ¼ yds from each cut (3) 6" squares (12) 2½" x 3¼"
Nests and Birds	2¾ yds	10 Different ½ yds	10 Different ½ yds
Nests	(8) 7" strips cut into 　(40) 7" x 8"	from each cut (4) 7" x 8"	from each cut (4) 7" x 8"
Birds	(5) 6" strips cut into 　(30) 6" squares	(3) 6" squares	(3) 6" squares
Edge Triangles	¾ yd (6) 10½" squares (2) 6" squares	¾ yd (6) 10½" squares (2) 6" squares	¾ yd (6) 10½" squares (2) 6" squares
First Border	⅔ yd (7) 2½" strips	⅔ yd (7) 2½" strips	⅔ yd (7) 2½" strips
Second Border			
Simple	⅔ yd (7) 2½" strips	⅔ yd (7) 2½" strips	⅔ yd (7) 2½" strips
Or			
Sawtooth Background	⅔ yd (3) 6" strips cut into 　(16) 6" squares (4) 2½" squares	⅔ yd (3) 6" strips cut into 　(16) 6" squares (4) 2½" squares	From above ¼ yds (16) 6" squares (4) 2½" squares
Birds	⅔ yd (3) 6" strips cut into 　(16) 6" squares	From above ½ yds (16) 6" squares	From above ½ yds (16) 6" squares
Third Border	¾ yd (7) 3½" strips	¾ yd (7) 3½" strips	¾ yd (7) 3½" strips
Fourth Border	1¾ yds (9) 5½" strips	1¾ yds (9) 5½" strips	1¾ yds (9) 5½" strips
Binding	1 yd (9) 3" strips	1 yd (9) 3" strips	1 yd (9) 3" strips
Backing	74" x 108"	74" x 108"	74" x 108"
Batting	74" x 108"	74" x 108"	74" x 108"

Twin Quilt

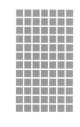

	Two Fabrics	One Background Multi-Fabric Nests and Birds	Multi-Fabric Background, Nests and Birds

Background	**2 yds**
	(6) 6" strips cut into
	    (33) 6" squares
	(11) 2½" strips cut into
	    (132) 2½" x 3¼"
		2 yds
		(6) 6" strips cut into
		    (33) 6" squares
		(11) 2½" strips cut into
		    (132) 2½" x 3¼"
			11 Different ¼ yds
			from each cut
			(3) 6" squares
			(12) 2½" x 3¼"

Nests and Birds	**3 yds**	**11 Different ½ yds**	**11 Different ½ yds**
Nests	(9) 7" strips cut into (44) 7" x 8"	from each cut (4) 7" x 8"	from each cut (4) 7" x 8"
Birds	(6) 6" strips cut into (33) 6" squares	(3) 6" squares	(3) 6" squares
First Border	**⅔ yd** (7) 2½" strips	**⅔ yd** (7) 2½" strips	**⅔ yd** (7) 2½" strips
Second Border			
Simple	**⅔ yd** (7) 2½" strips	**⅔ yd** (7) 2½" strips	**⅔ yd** (7) 2½" strips
Or			

Sawtooth
    Background
	⅔ yd
	(3) 6" strips cut into
	    (16) 6" squares
	(4) 2½" squares
		⅔ yd
		(3) 6" strips cut into
		    (16) 6" squares
		(4) 2½" squares
			From above ¼ yds
			(16) 6" squares
			(4) 2½" squares

Birds	**⅔ yd** (3) 6" strips cut into (16) 6" squares	**From above ½ yds** (16) 6" squares	**From above ½ yds** (16) 6" squares
Third Border	**1 yd** (8) 3½" strips	**1 yd** (8) 3½" strips	**1 yd** (8) 3½" strips
Fourth Border	**1½ yds** (9) 5½" strips	**1½ yds** (9) 5½" strips	**1½ yds** (9) 5½" strips
Binding	**1 yd** (9) 3" strips	**1 yd** (9) 3" strips	**1 yd** (9) 3" strips
Backing	**74" x 104"**	**74" x 104"**	**74" x 104"**
Batting	**74" x 104"**	**74" x 104"**	**74" x 104"**

Queen Quilt

	Two Fabrics	One Background Multi-Fabric Nests and Birds	Multi-Fabric Background, Nests and Birds

Background	**3 yds**
	(8) 6" strips cut into
	    (48) 6" squares
	(16) 2½" strips cut into
	    (192) 2½" x 3¼"
		3 yds
		(8) 6" strips cut into
		    (48) 6" squares
		(16) 2½" strips cut into
		    (192) 2½" x 3¼"
			16 Different ¼ yds
			from each cut
			(3) 6" squares
			(12) 2½" x 3¼"

Nests and Birds	**3¼ yds**	**16 Different ½ yds**	**16 Different ½ yds**
Nests	(13) 7" strips cut into (64) 7" x 8"	from each cut (4) 7" x 8"	from each cut (4) 7" x 8"
Birds	(8) 6" strips cut into (48) 6" squares	(3) 6" squares	(3) 6" squares
Edge Triangles	**1 yd** (8) 10½" squares (2) 6" squares	**1 yd** (8) 10½" squares (2) 6" squares	**1 yd** (8) 10½" squares (2) 6" squares
First Border	**1 yd** (8) 3¼" strips	**1 yd** (8) 3¼" strips	**1 yd** (8) 3¼" strips
Second Border			
Simple	**¾ yd** (8) 2½" strips	**¾ yd** (8) 2½" strips	**¾ yd** (8) 2½" strips
Or			

Sawtooth
  Background
	¾ yd
	(4) 6" strips cut into
	    (20) 6" squares
	(4) 2½" squares
		¾ yd
		(4) 6" strips cut into
		    (20) 6" squares
		(4) 2½" squares
			From above ¼ yds
			(20) 6" squares
			(4) 2½" squares

Birds	**¾ yd** (4) 6" strips cut into (20) 6" squares	**From above ½ yds** (20) 6" squares	**From above ½ yds** (20) 6" squares
Third Border	**1 yd** (9) 3½" strips	**1 yd** (9) 3½" strips	**1 yd** (9) 3½" strips
Fourth Border	**2 yds** (10) 5½" strips	**2 yds** (10) 5½" strips	**2 yds** (10) 5½" strips
Binding	**1 yd** (10) 3" strips	**1 yd** (10) 3" strips	**1 yd** (10) 3" strips
Backing	**92" x 118"**	**92" x 118"**	**92" x 118"**
Batting	**92" x 118"**	**92" x 118"**	**92" x 118"**

Queen Quilt

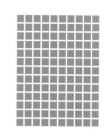

	Two Fabrics	One Background Multi-Fabric Nests and Birds	Multi-Fabric Background, Nests and Birds

Background	3 yds
	(9) 6" strips cut into
	    (51) 6" squares
	(17) 2½" strips cut into
	    (204) 2½" x 3¼"
		3 yds
		(9) 6" strips cut into
		    (51) 6" squares
		(17) 2 ½" strips cut into
		    (204) 2½" x 3¼"
			17 Different ¼ yds
			from each cut
			(3) 6" squares
			(12) 2½" x 3¼"

Nests and Birds
  Nests
 	
  Birds
	4½ yds
	(14) 7" strips cut into
	    (68) 7" x 8"
	(9) 6" strips cut into
	    (51) 6" squares
		17 Different ½ yds
		from each cut
		(4) 7" x 8"
		(3) 6" squares
			17 Different ½ yds
			from each cut
			(4) 7" x 8"
			(3) 6" squares

First Border	⅔ yd (8) 2½" strips	⅔ yd (8) 2½" strips	⅔ yd (8) 2½" strips
Second Border Simple	⅔ yd (8) 2½" strips	⅔ yd (8) 2½" strips	⅔ yd (8) 2½" strips
Or			

Sawtooth
  Background
	¾ yd
	(4) 6" strips cut into
	    (19) 6" squares
	(4) 2½" squares
		¾ yd
		(4) 6" strips cut into
		    (19) 6" squares
		(4) 2½" squares
			From above ¼ yds
			(19) 6" squares
			(4) 2½" squares

Birds	¾ yd (4) 6" strips cut into (19) 6" squares	From above ½ yds (19) 6" squares	From above ½ yds (19) 6" squares
Third Border	1 yd (9) 3½" strips	1 yd (9) 3½" strips	1 yd (9) 3½" strips
Fourth Border	2 yds (10) 5½" strips	2 yds (10) 5½" strips	2 yds (10) 5½" strips
Binding	1 yd (10) 3" strips	1 yd (10) 3" strips	1 yd (10) 3" strips
Backing	92" x 110"	92" x 110"	92" x 110"
Batting	92" x 110"	92" x 110"	92" x 110"

King Quilt

	Two Fabrics	One Background Multi-Fabric Nests and Birds	Multi-Fabric Background, Nests and Birds
Background	**4 yds** (12) 6" strips cut into (69) 6" squares (23) 2½" strips cut into (276) 2½" x 3¼"	**4 yds** (12) 6" strips cut into (69) 6" squares (23) 2½" strips cut into (276) 2½" x 3¼"	**23 Different ¼ yds** from each cut (3) 6" squares (12) 2½" x 3¼"

Nests and Birds
   Nests
 	
   Birds
	6 yds
	(19) 7" strips cut into
	(92) 7" x 8"
	(12) 6" strips cut into
	(69) 6" squares
		23 Different ½ yds
		from each cut
		(4) 7" x 8"
		(3) 6" squares
			23 Different ½ yds
			from each cut
			(4) 7" x 8"
			(3) 6" squares

Edge Triangles	**1 yd** (9) 10½" squares (2) 6" squares	**1 yd** (9) 10½" squares (2) 6" squares	**1 yd** (9) 10½" squares (2) 6" squares
First Border	**1 yd** (10) 3¼" strips	**1 yd** (10) 3¼" strips	**1 yd** (10) 3¼" strips
Second Border Simple Or	**1 yd** (11) 2½" strips	**1 yd** (11) 2½" strips	**1 yd** (11) 2½" strips
Sawtooth Background	**¾ yd** (4) 6" strips cut into (23) 6" squares (4) 2½" squares	**¾ yd** (4) 6" strips cut into (23) 6" squares (4) 2½" squares	**From above ¼ yds** (23) 6" squares (4) 2½" squares
Birds	**¾ yd** (4) 6" strips cut into (23) 6" squares	**From above ½ yds** (23) 6" squares	**From above ½ yds** (23) 6" squares
Third Border	**1¼ yds** (11) 3½" strips	**1¼ yds** (11) 3½" strips	**1¼ yds** (11) 3½" strips
Fourth Border	**2¼ yds** (12) 5½" strips	**2¼ yds** (12) 5½" strips	**2¼ yds** (12) 5½" strips
Binding	**1¼ yds** (12) 3" strips	**1¼ yds** (12) 3" strips	**1¼ yds** (12) 3" strips
Backing	**118" x 118"**	**118" x 118"**	**118" x 118"**
Batting	**118" x 118"**	**118" x 118"**	**118" x 118"**

King Quilt

	Two Fabrics	One Background **Multi-Fabric Nests and Birds**	Multi-Fabric **Background, Nests and Birds**

Background	4½ yds
	(13) 6" strips cut into
	   (75) 6" squares
	(25) 2½" strips cut into
	   (300) 2½" x 3¼"
		4½ yds
		(13) 6" strips cut into
		   (75) 6" squares
		(25) 2½" strips cut into
		   (300) 2½" x 3¼"
			25 Different ¼ yds
			from each cut
			(3) 6" squares
			(12) 2½" x 3¼"

Nests and Birds	6½ yds	25 Different ½ yds	25 Different ½ yds
Nest	(20) 7" strips cut into (100) 7" x 8"	from each cut (4) 7" x 8"	from each cut (4) 7" x 8"
Birds	(13) 6" strips cut into (75) 6" squares	(3) 6" squares	(3) 6" squares
First Border	¾ yd (9) 2½" strips	¾ yd (9) 2½" strips	¾ yd (9) 2½" strips
Second Border			
Simple	¾ yd (10) 2½" strips	¾ yd (10) 2½" strips	¾ yd (11) 2½" strips
Or			

Sawtooth
  Background
	¾ yd
	(4) 6" strips cut into
	   (22) 6" squares
	(4) 2½" squares
		¾ yd
		(4) 6" strips cut into
		   (22) 6" squares
		(4) 2½" squares
			From above ¼ yds
			(22) 6" squares
			(4) 2½" squares

Birds	¾ yd (4) 6" strips cut into (22) 6" squares	From above ½ yds (22) 6" squares	From above ½ yds (22) 6" squares
Third Border	1¼ yds (10) 3½" strips	1¼ yds (10) 3½" strips	1¼ yds (10) 3½" strips
Fourth Border	2 yds (11) 5½" strips	2 yds (11) 5½" strips	2 yds (11) 5½" strips
Binding	1 yd (11) 3" strips	1 yd (11) 3" strips	1 yd (11) 3" strips
Backing	116" x 116"	116" x 116"	116" x 116"
Batting	116" x 116"	116" x 116"	116" x 116"

Cutting and Sewing

Cutting Strips and Squares

1. Press fabric.

2. Fold fabric in half, matching edges. Don't worry about the selvages lining up correctly as this is not always possible.

3. Lay fabric on cutting mat with most of it to the right. Make sure edge is lined up at the left. Lay the ¼" line on 6" x 24" ruler along edge, and straighten.

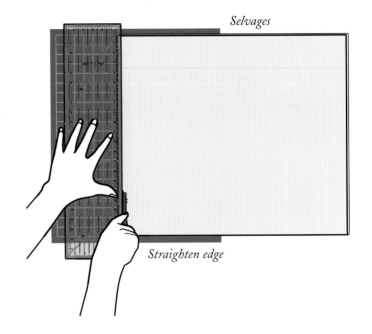

Selvages

Straighten edge

4. Reposition ruler, and line up designated strip width. Cut Background and Bird strips 6" wide with ruler. Cut Nest strips 7" wide using cutting mat lines.

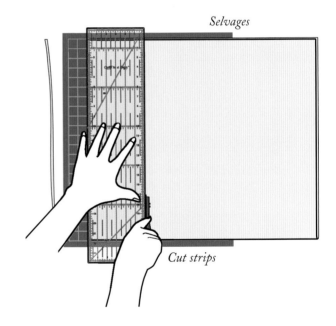

Selvages

Cut strips

5. Turn strip and square off selvage edges. Layer cut Background and Birds into 6" squares and Nests into 7" x 8" rectangles. Rectangles from Background are 2½" strips cut into 2½" x 3¼".

6. Repeat until you have the desired number of strips, squares, and rectangles.

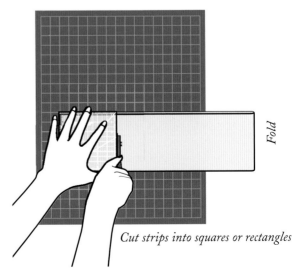

Fold

Cut strips into squares or rectangles

Cutting Multi-Fabric Background, Nests and Birds

If your chart specifies ¼ or ½ yard pieces for Background, Nests and Birds, cut pieces for the blocks according to your yardage chart.

Multi-Fabric Wallhangings

For every two blocks, cut ¼ yd Background into one 6" square and three 2½" x 3¼" small rectangles. It is important to cut these small rectangles accurately.

¼ yard Background for two blocks

For every two blocks, cut ¼ yd piece into one 6" square for Birds and one 7" x 8" rectangle for Nests.

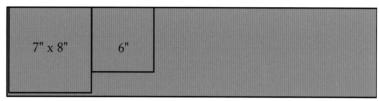
¼ yard Nests and Birds for two blocks

If you want a Sawtooth Border, cut the required number of 6" squares from the leftovers.

Larger Quilts

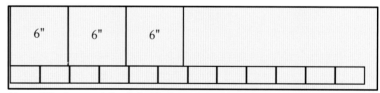
¼ yard Background for eight blocks

For every eight blocks, cut ¼ yd Background into three 6" squares and twelve 2½" x 3¼" small rectangles.

For every eight blocks, cut ½ yd piece into three 6" squares for Birds and four 7" x 8" rectangles for Nests.

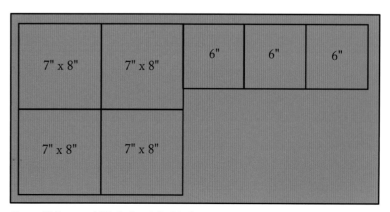
½ yard Nests and Birds for eight blocks

25

Getting Prepared – Organizing Your Pieces

In all quilts, four Two Block Patches are made at a time and cut in half for eight blocks. Save valuable time by pre-packaging pieces. The Multi-Fabric Wallhangings are the exception with only one Two Block Patch made at a time for variety.

Pre-packaging Pieces for Eight Blocks
Count out pieces and place in individual plastic bags.

Background
(3) 6" squares
(12) 2½" x 3¼" rectangles

Bird Fabric
(3) 6" squares

Nest Fabric
(4) 7" x 8" rectangles

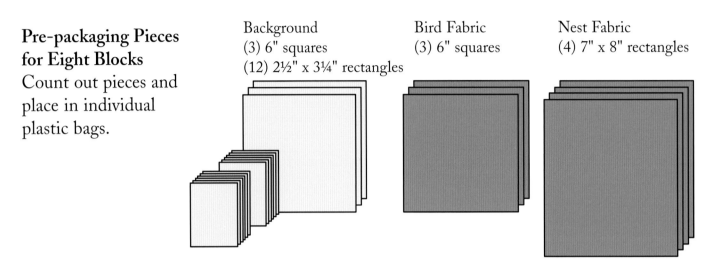

Number of Packages					
	Two Fabric Wallhanging	Lap	Twin	Queen	King
On Point	2	8	10	16	23
Set Straight	2	8	11	17	25

Pre-packaging Pieces for Two Blocks
Count out pieces and place in individual plastic bags.
Each set has two left over Birds for the Sawtooth Border.

Number of Packages	
Multi-Fabric Wallhangings	
On Point	7
Set Straight	8

Background
(1) 6" square
(3) 2½" x 3¼" rectangles

Bird Fabric
(1) 6" square

Nest Fabric
(1) 7" x 8" rectangle

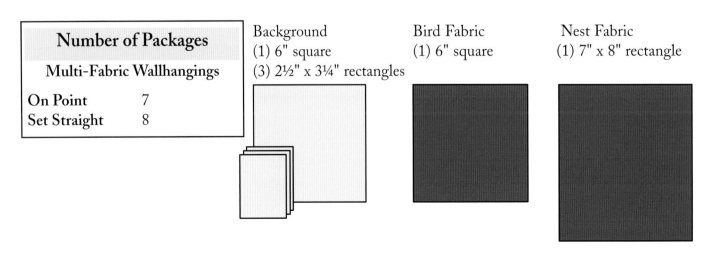

¼" Seam Test

Take the ¼" seam test before starting.
Use a consistent ¼" seam throughout construction of the quilt. Sew 15 stitches to the inch or a setting of 2.0.

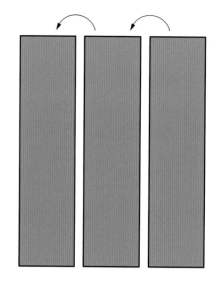

1. Cut (3) 1½" x 6" pieces, and sew the three strips together lengthwise with what you think is a perfect ¼" seam.

2. Press the seams in one direction. Make sure no folds occur at the seam when pressing.

3. Place the sewn sample under a ruler and measure its width. It should measure exactly 3½". If sample measures smaller than 3½", seam is too large. If sample measures larger than 3½", seam is too small.

4. Correct the seam by adjusting the needle position, changing the presser foot, or feeding the fabric under the presser foot to achieve the ¼" seam.

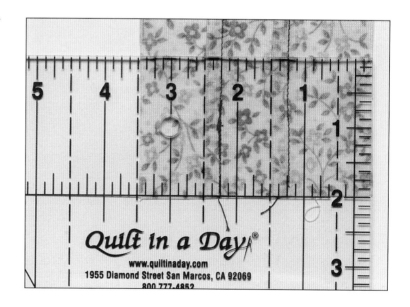

Making Birds

Multi-Fabric Wallhangings are in blue text.

1. From one package, select three 6" squares of the **same Background** and three 6" squares of the **same Birds**.

   Multi-Fabric Wallhangings: One 6" square of Background and Birds.

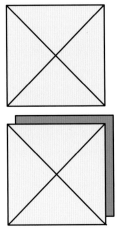

2. With a fine point permanent marking pen, draw diagonal lines on the wrong side of each Background square.

3. Place marked Background squares right sides together with Birds squares. Pin.

4. Set up machine with thread that shows against the wrong side of both fabrics. It is important to see the stitching.

5. Sew exactly ¼" from the line with 15 stitches to the inch or a setting of 2.0.

6. Chain sew paired squares.

7. Turn chain. Chain sew ¼" from other side of line. Clip apart.

8. Measure distance between two lines of stitching. **It should be no wider than ½".**

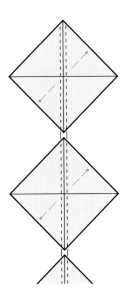

9. Repeat chain sewing on both sides of other line. Clip apart.

10. Press to set seams.

11. Lay out one sewn 6" square on cutting mat. Line up with grid lines.

12. Without moving squares, cut horizontally and vertically at 3". Use 6" x 12" ruler.

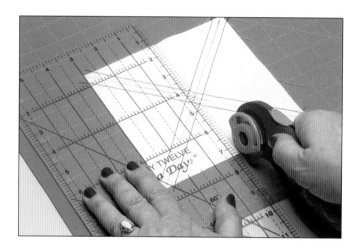

13. Cut on both diagonal lines.

14. Repeat with remaining 6" squares. There should be a total of 24 closed triangles.

Multi-Fabric Wallhangings: Eight closed triangles.

15. Stack closed triangles dark or light side up, which ever side shows the thread.

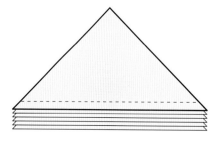

Squaring Up One Test Triangle to 2½"

Triangles are oversized and need to be trimmed to 2½". This technique is called "squaring up."

Use the Quilt in a Day 6½" Triangle Square Up ruler, or Six by Twelve ruler with red diagonal lines.

Skip to page 32 for instructions using the 6" Square Up ruler.

6½" Triangle
Square Up Ruler

6" x 12" Ruler

The example shows squaring with the 6½" Triangle Square Up ruler.

1. **Lay one test triangle on the cutting mat.**

   Look for uneven edges. Freshly cut edges don't need trimmed.

2. Lay the ruler's red dashed 2½" line **on** the stitching line.

3. Line up top edge of ruler with triangle. Hold ruler firmly.

4. Trim side of triangle, pushing rotary cutter toward the point to avoid damaging the ruler's corner.

5. Turn patch. Trim tips with rotary cutter and ruler. From stitching, trim a 45° angle.

6. Tips can also be trimmed with scissors, using a 60° angle to assure that seam allowance does not show after triangle is pressed open.

   Optional: You can also trim tips after pieced square is pressed open.

7. Lay trimmed triangle on pressing mat, **Bird side up.** Lift corner and press toward seam with tip of iron, **pushing seams to Bird side**. Press carefully so test pieced square does not distort.

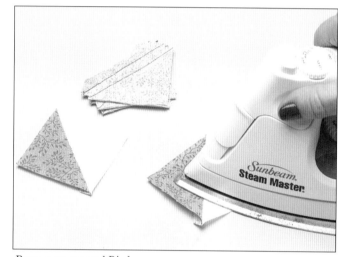

Press seam toward Bird

8. Lay pieced square on cutting mat. Lay 6" Square Up ruler on opened pieced square to see if it measures 2½" square.

9. If pieced square measures a perfect 2½" square, repeat steps with all remaining triangles.

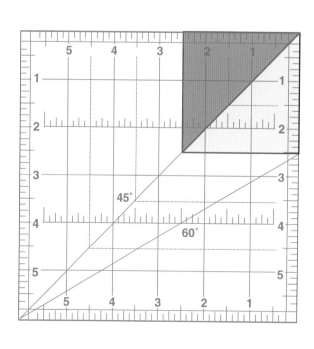

Making Adjustments

If pieced square is not a perfect 2½", make an adjustment before trimming remaining triangles.

1. Lay out a new triangle.

2. Lay the 6½" Triangle Square Up ruler's 2½" red dashed line **below** the stitching for a smaller pieced square, and **above** the stitching for a larger pieced square. Stitching and ruler line should touch.

3. Trim and measure again.

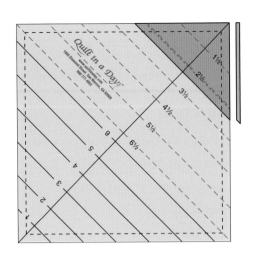

Squaring with a 6" Square Up Ruler

If you have a Quilt in a Day **6" Square Up Ruler** to trim, use this method.

1. Drop triangle on pressing mat with **Bird fabric** on top. Press to set seam.

2. Open and **press seam toward Bird.**

3. Place 6" Square Up ruler on pieced square so 2½" is centered on patch. Trim on two sides.

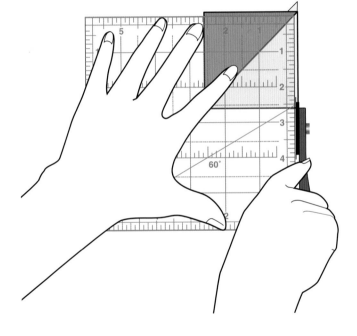

4. Turn and place 2½" line on cut edges. Cut remaining two sides, squaring patch.

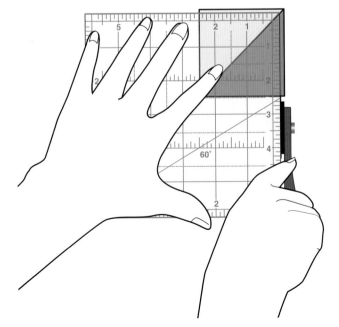

Making Three Stacks of Birds

Each stack becomes a designated part of the finished Patch.

Eight Identical Blocks

For eight identical blocks, place twelve in one stack,
four in one stack, and eight in one stack.

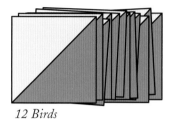

12 Birds

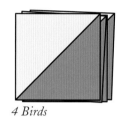

4 Birds

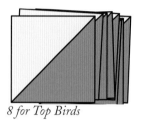

8 for Top Birds

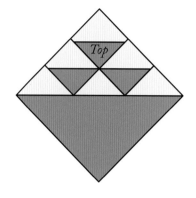

Creative Birds

If you want Top Birds to be a different fabric,
place in the stack of eight. *(See page 72 for example)*

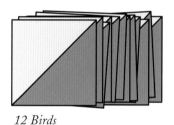

12 Birds

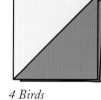

4 Birds

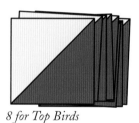

8 for Top Birds

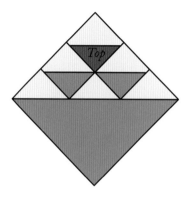

Multi-Fabric Wallhangings

For two identical blocks, place three in one stack, one in one
stack, and two in one stack. There are two extra Birds.

3 Birds

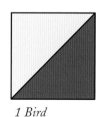

1 Bird

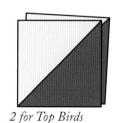

2 for Top Birds

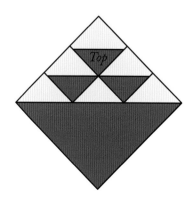

Sewing Birds Together

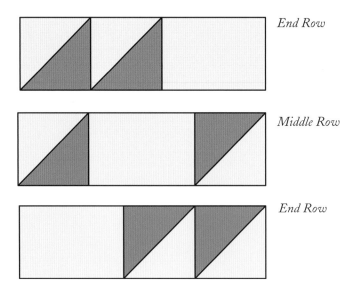

End Row

Middle Row

End Row

There are three rows in the Two Block Patch. Each row has a 2½" x 3¼" rectangle.

1. Count out (12) 2½" x 3¼" rectangles **matching Background of Birds.**

2. Lay stack of **12 rectangles** with stack of **12 Birds. Birds point downward next to rectangle.**

   Multi-Fabric Wallhangings: Three rectangles and three Birds.

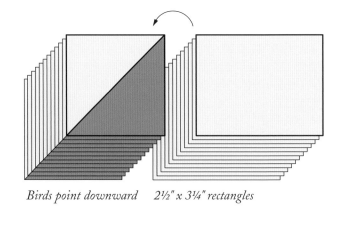

Birds point downward   *2½" x 3¼" rectangles*

3. Flip rectangle right sides together to Bird, matching edges. Chain sew 12 pairs.

   Multi-Fabric Wallhangings: Three pairs.

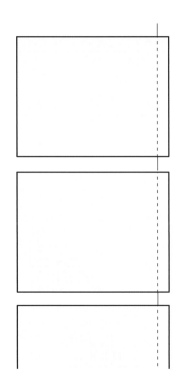

4. **Do not clip apart.** Set seam with rectangle on top, open, and press against seam, pushing seams to rectangle.

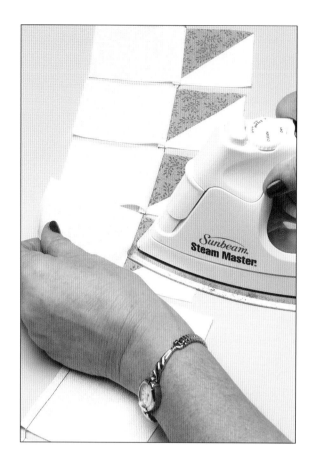

5. **Clip into chain of four and chain of eight.** Set aside the eight for End Rows, page 38.

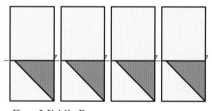

Four Middle Rows

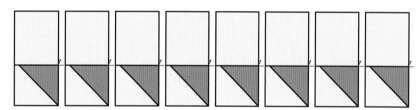

Eight End Rows

Multi-Fabric Wallhangings:
Clip into one and chain of two. Set aside two for End Rows.

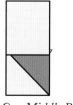
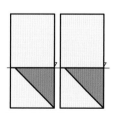

One Middle Row   *Two End Rows*

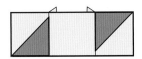

Making Four Middle Rows

Multi-Fabric Wallhangings:
Making One Middle Row

1. Place **four** chained pieces on left, wrong side up, and stack of four Birds in arm of sewing machine, **right side up.**

2. Slide Bird under rectangle.

Multi-Fabric Wallhangings:
One pair with one Bird.

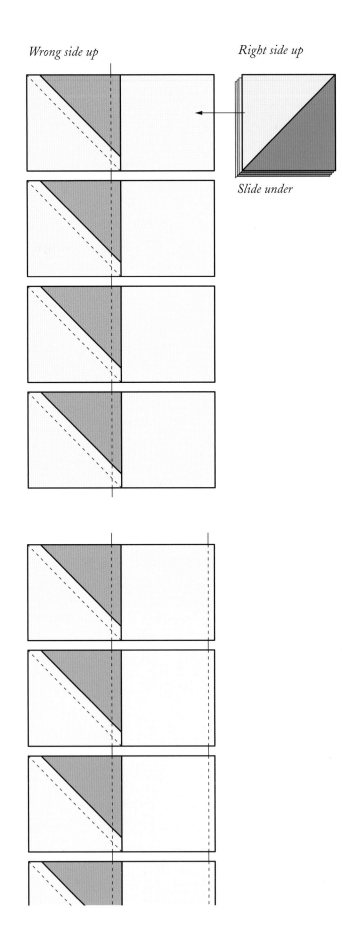

Wrong side up   *Right side up*

Slide under

3. Chain sew four pieces.

Multi-Fabric Wallhangings:
Sew one Middle Row.

4. Do not clip apart. Lay on pressing mat with rectangle on top, and set seam.

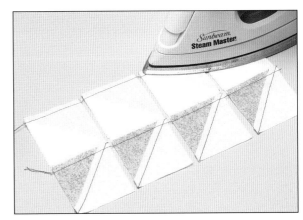

5. Open, and press against seam, pushing seams to rectangle. Clip apart. **Seams are pressed toward middle.**

Seams are pressed toward middle

6. Stack and set aside these four Middle Rows.

Multi-Fabric Wallhangings:
Set aside one Middle Row.

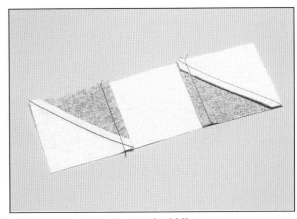

Seams pressed correctly toward middle

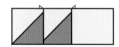 **Making Eight End Rows**

Multi-Fabric Wallhangings:
Making Two End Rows

1. Select chain of eight Birds with
   rectangles and stack of eight Birds.

   This stack of eight becomes the Top Bird.

2. Place chained pieces on left, wrong side
   up, and stack of eight pieced squares in
   arm of sewing machine, right side up.

3. Slide Bird under Bird and chain sew
   eight pieces.

   Multi-Fabric Wallhangings: Sew two
   chained pieces with two Birds.

   This stack of two becomes the Top Bird.

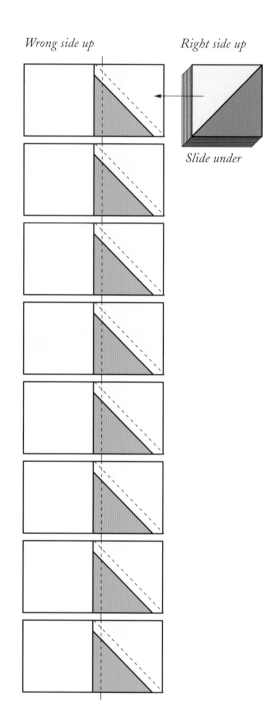

Wrong side up   *Right side up*

Slide under

4. **Do not clip apart.**

5. Lay on pressing mat. Set seams with newly added Bird on top.

6. Open each and press against seam, pushing seams to newly added Bird.

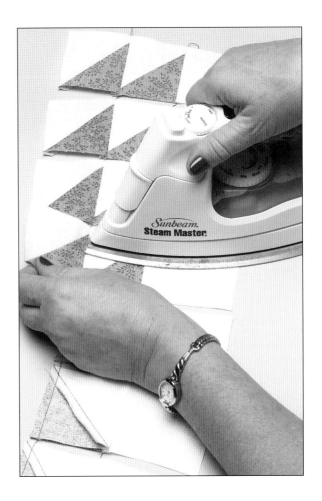

7. Clip apart. **Check all pieces are turned and pressed correctly.**

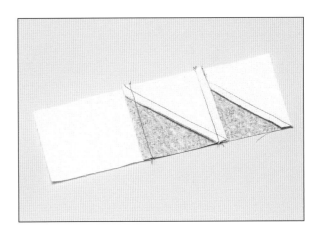

8. Make two stacks of End Rows with four in each.

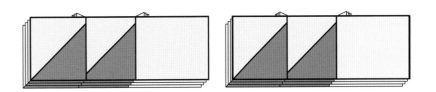

Sewing Rows Together

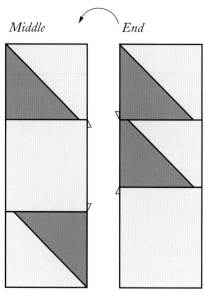

Middle   *End*

1. Lay out stack of four Middle Rows and stack of four End Rows.

Multi-Fabric Wallhangings: One of each.

2. Flip End Row to Middle Row.

Lower seams do not meet

3. Pin or finger pin top seams so they meet and lock. **The lower seams don't meet.**

4. Be careful that underneath seam does not flip. **Hold seams with stiletto, and sew over seams as pressed.** Match bottom edges.

5. Chain sew four pieces.

6. **Do not press.**

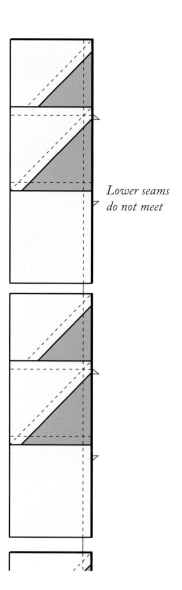

Lower seams do not meet

7. Finger press open. See circles on front
   and back where lower seams don't meet.

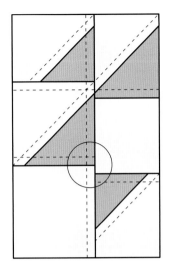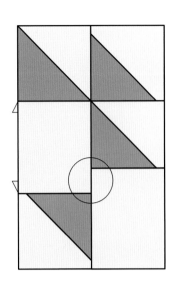

8. Turn chain around.

9. Lay out remaining stack of End Rows
   next to Middle Rows.

Multi-Fabric Wallhangings: One Row.

10. Flip End Row to Middle Row. Pin or
    finger pin top seams so they meet and
    lock. **The lower seams don't meet.**

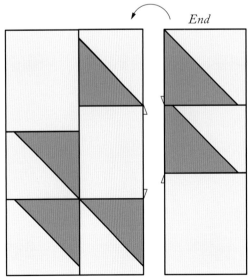

Sew over seams as they were pressed

11. **Chain sew over seams as they were pressed.** Match bottom edges.

Multi-Fabric Wallhangings: One Row.

12. Clip patches apart. **Do not press yet.**

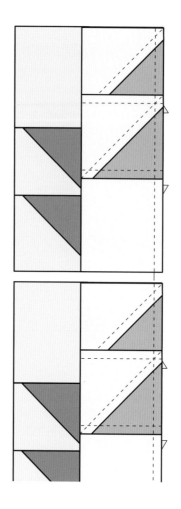

Pressing the Patches

1. **On the front,** notice in the circles that there are gaps between Birds.

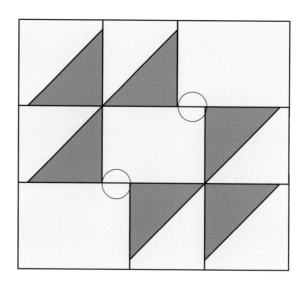

2. **On the back,** seams in those gaps are clipped to the stitching in order to press seams in the directions of the arrows.

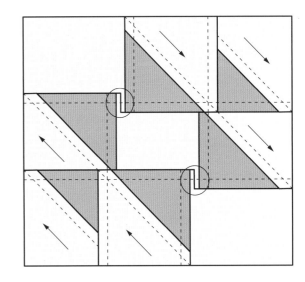

3. Use sharp scissors to clip to the stitching in gaps.

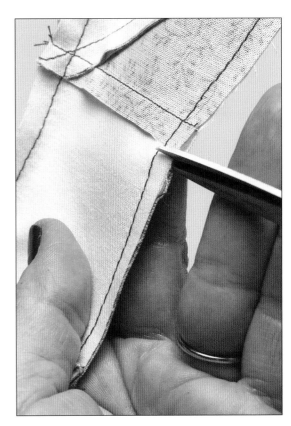

4. Press seams on the wrong side one half at a time from two Birds toward one Bird. Use a gridded pressing mat to help keep patch straight.

5. Pressing different directions can cause the patch to be "out of square." If it is "out of square," tug the corners to straighten the patch. Press again.

6. Measure your patch. It should be approximately 6½" x 7¼".

7. It is important that the patch is pressed with no folds or pleats at the seams.

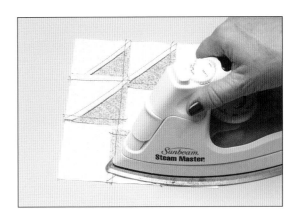

Marking the Patches

Mark your patches with a 6" x 12" ruler or 12" Quick Quarter ruler.

1. Lay patch wrong side up so you can see seams.

2. Place point of sharp #2 soft pencil at top corner. Do not use a permanent marking pen that may show through on right side.

3. Lay 6" x 12" ruler on patch. Shift ruler until its edge touches the pencil and "points" of the Birds. See red dots.

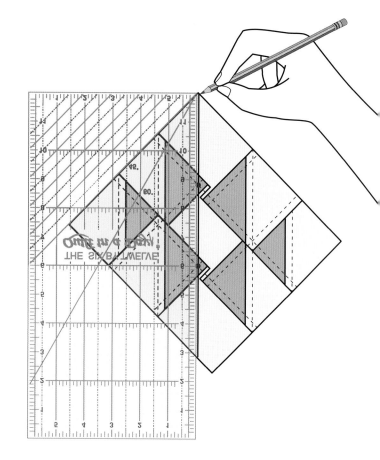

4. Draw a sewing line just to right of "points" from top corner to bottom edge. **Do not cut.**

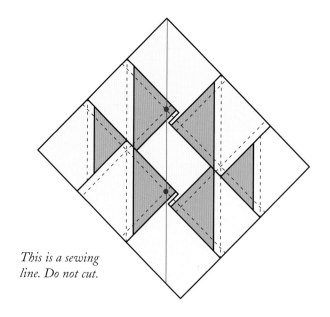

This is a sewing line. Do not cut.

5. Slide ruler over, and repeat match points.

6. **Draw a second sewing line just to left of "points."**

7. Mark remaining patches. **Sharpen pencil often.**

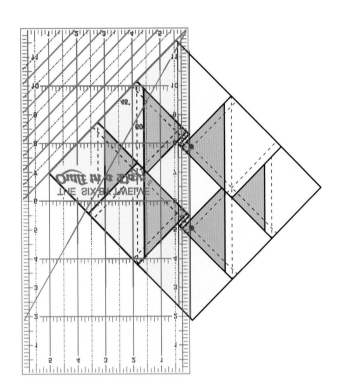

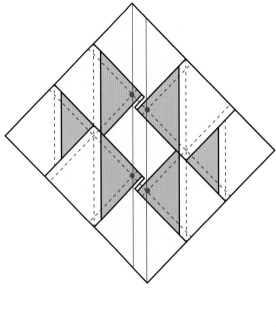

Second Marking Method

Use the Quick Quarter Ruler for marking sewing lines. It's a lightweight turquoise ruler 12" long and ½" wide with a slot down the center.

1. Place Quick Quarter II ruler on block. Place ruler so edges touch "points" of seams. Ruler's top left edge should line up with top corner, and ruler's bottom right edge should line up with bottom corner.

2. Draw light pencil lines on both sides of ruler. These lines are sewing lines.

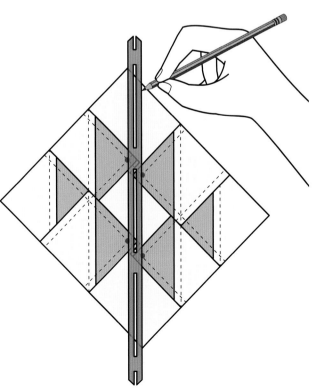

Making Two Block Patches

1. Count out **four matching 7" x 8"** Nest rectangles.

   Multi-Fabric Wallhangings:
   One matching 7" x 8" Nest rectangle.

2. Center marked patches right sides together on rectangles. Pin securely.

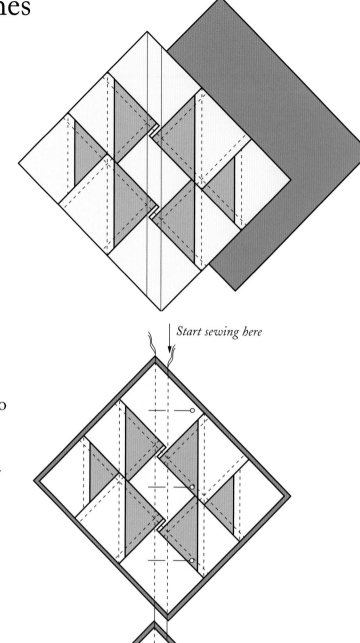

3. **Change to multi-purpose presser foot or open toe foot.**

4. Chain sew **on** marked line. Use stiletto to hold seams flat.

   If necessary, sew on left side of line so points remain "crisp."

Start sewing here

5. Turn chain around and sew on second marked line.

6. Clip apart.

7. Press on both sides to set seams.

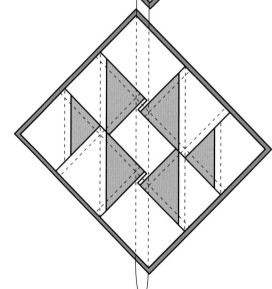

8. Rotary cut between stitching.

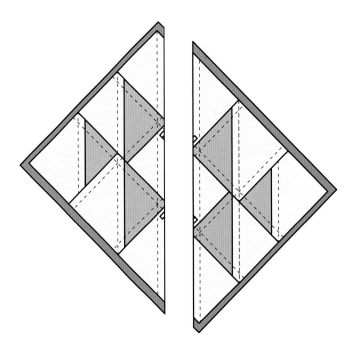

9. Place closed block on pressing mat with Nest side up.
   Set seam, open, and press seams toward Nest.

10. Continue to make sets of Two Block Patches until you have the total number of blocks needed for your quilt.

Number of Blocks	
Multi-Fabric Wallhanging	
On Point	13
Set Straight	16
Extra Blocks	
On Point	1
Set Straight	0

Number of Blocks				
Two Fabric Wallhanging	Lap	Twin	Queen	King
On Point 13	59	77	124	181
Set Straight 16	60	84	130	196
Extra Blocks				
On Point 3	5	3	4	3
Set Straight 0	4	4	6	4

Determining the Size of Your Blocks

1. Lay pressed open block on cutting mat. Using the 6" x 12" Ruler, measure Bird side of block. Typical sides are 6½", 6⅜", or 6¼". Measure several.

   Record measurement _____.

2. **Nests are squared to this measurement.** When you've determined the size of your blocks, **trim all Nests to this size** with 6½" Triangle Square Up ruler or 12½" Square Up ruler, page 51.

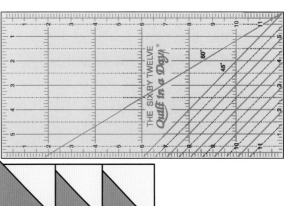

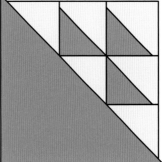

Measure side of Birds

Squaring Blocks with Triangle Square Up

1. Lay the Triangle Square Up ruler on the block with the 6½" ruler line on the center seam. Green numbers 1-6 on ruler should be on Nest.

2. Ruler's diagonal line should go through center of Birds. If necessary, pull slightly to straighten. Even if Birds are not perfect, blocks sew together!

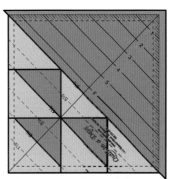

For 6½" block, lay 6½" diagonal line on seam

3. If your Bird side measured 6½", trim Nest to 6½". **Do not trim Birds**.

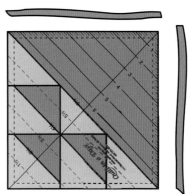

Trim Nest only

4. If your Bird side measured 6⅜", slide the ruler and line up the 6⅜" lines on the ends of the seam line. Keeping the 6½" line parallel with the seam lines, trim Nest. The ruler will extend beyond the Birds evenly.

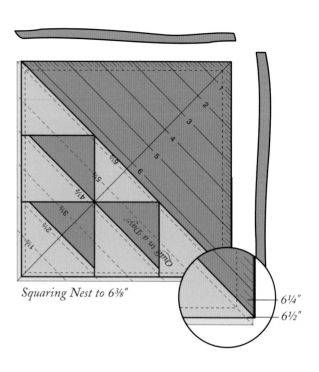

Squaring Nest to 6⅜"

5. If your side measured 6¼", slide the ruler and line up the 6¼" lines on the ends of the seam line. Trim Nest. The ruler will extend beyond the Birds evenly.

6. Repeat process with remaining pieces. Trim all blocks to the same size.

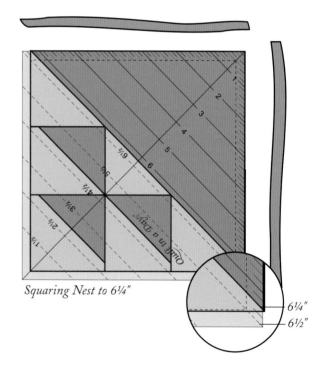

Squaring Nest to 6¼"

Squaring Blocks with 12½" Square Up

1. Place block on cutting mat with Nest in top right position. Place 12½" Square Up on block, lining up measurement of Bird side with top and right sides of Nest.

2. Ruler's diagonal line should go down center of Birds. If not, stretch block slightly. Even if Birds are not perfect at this step, blocks still sew together!

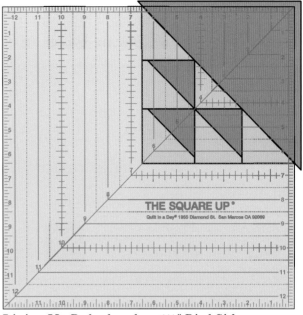

Lining Up Ruler based on 6½" Bird Side

3. **Trim Nest only** on two sides.

4. Trim all blocks to the same size.

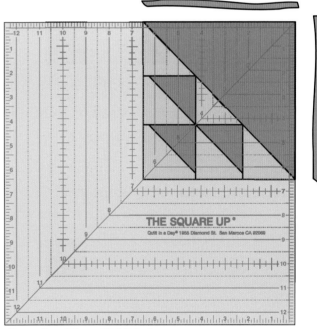

Squaring Up a 6½" Block

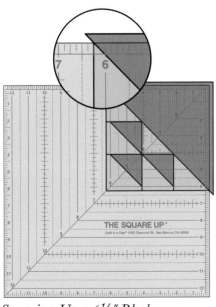

Squaring Up a 6¼" Block

On Point Setting

Edge and Corner Setting Triangles are oversized for easier sewing and trimming. Depending on your creativity, these triangles may be one fabric or a variety of fabrics.

Four Corner Triangles

The four corners are triangles with two "straight of the grain" outside edges.

1. Place two 6" squares on cutting mat.

2. Cut on one diagonal.

Edge Triangles

Four Edge Triangles are cut from a 10½" square. The long side of the triangle is on the "straight of the grain" and becomes the edge of the quilt.

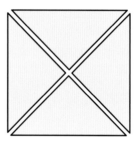

1. Place 10½" squares on cutting mat.

2. Cut on both diagonals with 6" x 24" ruler.

Alternate method

If you prefer, cut Edge Triangles from smaller pieces in a variety of fabrics.

1. Cut fabric into 5¼" x 11" pieces.

2. Finger press in half, and open.

3. Use 12½" Square Up Ruler. Line up diagonal line on fold.

4. Trim on both sides.

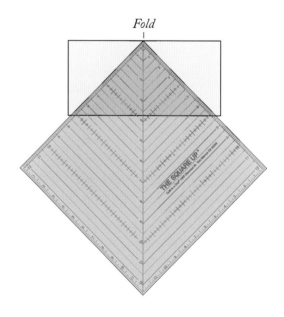

Fold

Sewing Multi-Fabric Blocks Together

1. On a bed or large area, lay out and arrange blocks according to your selected size. You may have extra blocks. See layouts on pages 54-55.

2. If using a variety of fabrics, arrange for pleasing color distribution.

Layout of Lap Robe

3. Lay Corner and Edge Triangles in place around the quilt.

Layout of Lap Robe

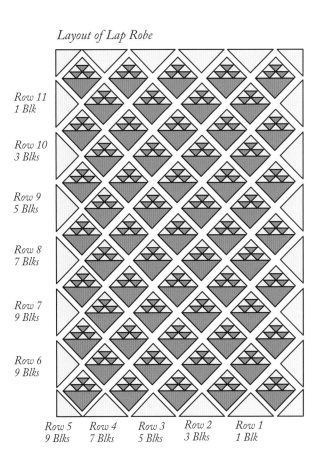

Row 11
1 Blk

Row 10
3 Blks

Row 9
5 Blks

Row 8
7 Blks

Row 7
9 Blks

Row 6
9 Blks

Row 5   *Row 4*   *Row 3*   *Row 2*   *Row 1*
9 Blks   *7 Blks*   *5 Blks*   *3 Blks*   *1 Blk*

Quilt Layouts

Sewing Two Fabric Blocks Together

It's not necessary to lay out identical blocks made from Two Fabrics.

1. Note the number of rows in your layout. Set aside that many single blocks.

2. Make two stacks with remaining blocks.

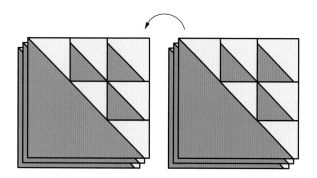

3. Flip right block to left block, and match outside edges. Assembly-line sew into pairs.

4. Referring to your layout, sew pairs and single blocks together for each row.

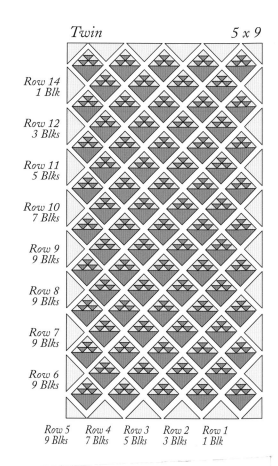

Twin   5 x 9

Row 14 1 Blk
Row 12 3 Blks
Row 11 5 Blks
Row 10 7 Blks
Row 9 9 Blks
Row 8 9 Blks
Row 7 9 Blks
Row 6 9 Blks

Row 5 9 Blks | Row 4 7 Blks | Row 3 5 Blks | Row 2 3 Blks | Row 1 1 Blk

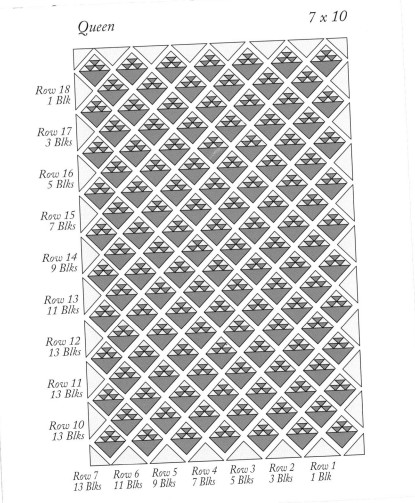

Queen   7 x 10

Row 18 1 Blk
Row 17 3 Blks
Row 16 5 Blks
Row 15 7 Blks
Row 14 9 Blks
Row 13 11 Blks
Row 12 13 Blks
Row 11 13 Blks
Row 10 13 Blks

Row 7 13 Blks | Row 6 11 Blks | Row 5 9 Blks | Row 4 7 Blks | Row 3 5 Blks | Row 2 3 Blks | Row 1 1 Blk

King   *10 x 10*

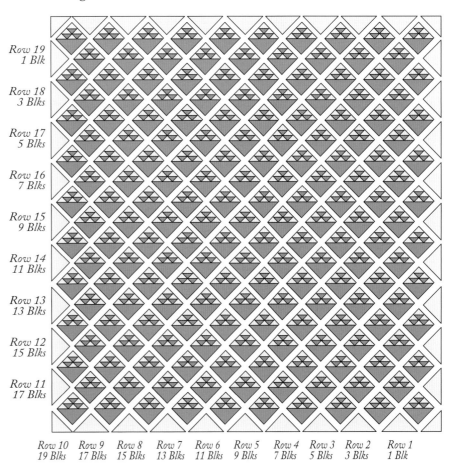

Row 19
1 Blk

Row 18
3 Blks

Row 17
5 Blks

Row 16
7 Blks

Row 15
9 Blks

Row 14
11 Blks

Row 13
13 Blks

Row 12
15 Blks

Row 11
17 Blks

Row 10 19 Blks	Row 9 17 Blks	Row 8 15 Blks	Row 7 13 Blks	Row 6 11 Blks	Row 5 9 Blks	Row 4 7 Blks	Row 3 5 Blks	Row 2 3 Blks	Row 1 1 Blk

Lap Robe   *5 x 7*

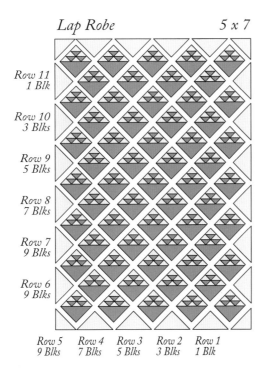

Row 11
1 Blk

Row 10
3 Blks

Row 9
5 Blks

Row 8
7 Blks

Row 7
9 Blks

Row 6
9 Blks

Row 5 9 Blks	Row 4 7 Blks	Row 3 5 Blks	Row 2 3 Blks	Row 1 1 Blk

Wallhanging   *3 x 3*

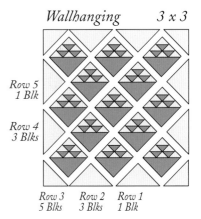

Row 5
1 Blk

Row 4
3 Blks

Row 3 5 Blks	Row 2 3 Blks	Row 1 1 Blk

Sewing Rows Together

Blocks are sewn in diagonal rows. Your quilt may have fewer or more rows than this Lap Robe.

1. Set aside three Corner Triangles to be added last.

Row 11

Row 10

Row 9

Row 8

Row 7

Row 6

Row 5

Row 4

Row 3

Row 2

Row 1

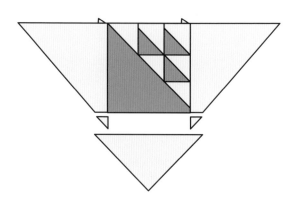

2. Starting at Row 1 on lower right corner of quilt, sew two Edge Triangles to corner block. Keep top edge even.

3. From wrong side, press seams in one direction to the left.

4. Trim exposed tips, and add Corner Triangle. Place back in layout.

5. Pin and sew Row 2 blocks and Side Triangles.

6. Continue to sew blocks and Side Triangles of each row together.

7. Press seams of odd numbered rows (1, 3, 5 etc.) to left, and seams of even numbered rows (2, 4, 6 etc.) to right.

8. Flip Row 1 to Row 2, matching and locking seams. Pin or finger pin. Sew.

9. Sew all rows together.

10. Press seams between rows in one direction.

11. Add final three Corners.

12. Trim excess of Edge and Corner Triangles evenly, leaving at least ¼" to a ⅜" seam allowance.

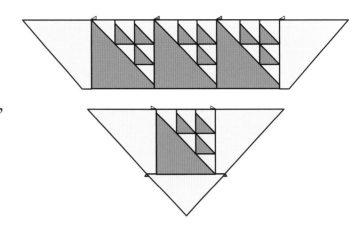

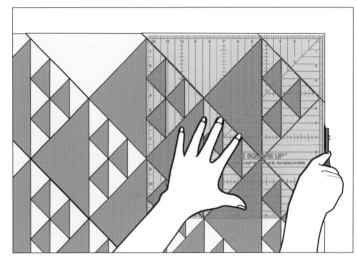

Use the 12½" or 16" Square Up ruler to trim the corners.

13. Press the quilt top.

14. Skip to Borders on page 60.

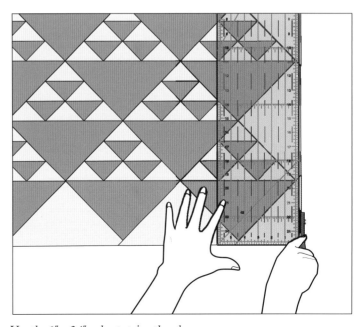

Use the 6" x 24" ruler to trim the edges.

Straight Setting

1. On a bed or large area, lay out and arrange blocks according to the chart. You may have extra blocks.

Blocks			
	Width		Length
Wallhanging	4	x	4
Lap	6	x	10
Twin	7	x	12
Queen	10	x	13
King	14	x	14

2. If using a variety of fabrics, arrange for pleasing color distribution.

3. Flip the second vertical row to the first vertical row, and stack pairs with top blocks remaining on top.

4. Match outside edges, and assembly-line sew pairs together. Use stiletto to hold seams flat. Do not clip apart.

5. Open Rows 1 and 2. Stack and add Row 3.

6. Sew all vertical rows for your size quilt.

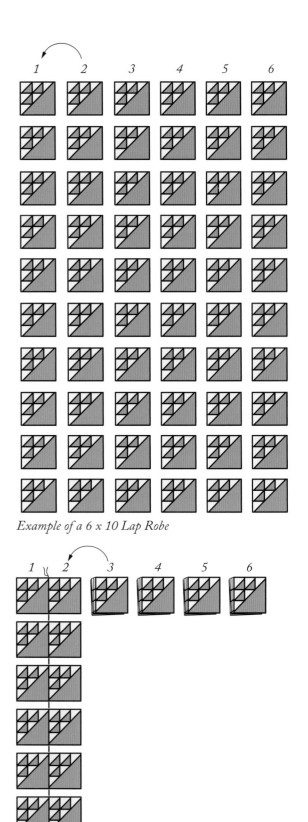

Example of a 6 x 10 Lap Robe

58

7. Turn chained rows, and sew horizontal rows. Push seams in opposite directions and lock at each intersection.

8. Keep previously sewn row on top, so vertical seams are pushed in same direction on both ends.

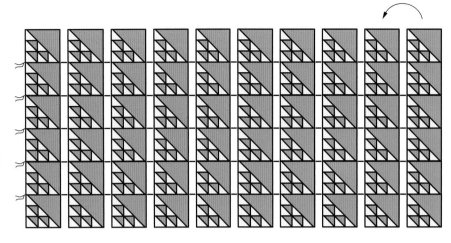

9. Press quilt top from wrong side. Turn and press from right side.

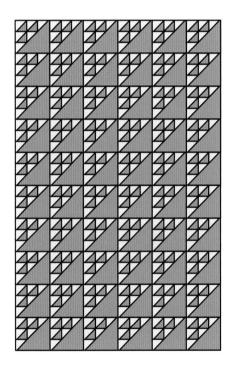

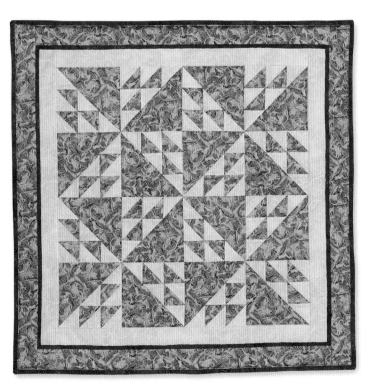

For an alternate Pinwheel arrangement, place groups of four blocks at a time.

Borders

Piecing Border Strips for Larger Quilts

1. Lay first strip right side up. Lay second strip right sides to it. Backstitch, stitch and back stitch again.

2. Continue assembly-line sewing all short ends together into one long piece.

Adding First Border

1. Cut two pieces the average length of left and right sides.

2. Pin and sew to sides. Set seams with Border on top. Open, and press seams toward Border.

3. Measure width and cut Border pieces for top and bottom.

4. Pin and sew to quilt. Set seams, and press toward Border.

5. Add remaining Borders, or Optional Sawtooth Second Border.

Optional Sawtooth Second Border

The Sawtooth Border is a strip of 2½" Pieced Squares between the First and Third Borders. It may run in one direction all around the quilt, or two directions on each side of the quilt, and may be used with blocks set straight or set on point.

1. Count out pairs of 6" squares of Background and Birds. Refer to charts below.

2. Make 2½" Birds following directions on pages 27 – 32.

3. Count out total needed into four stacks, making a stack for each side.

4. Choose either a Sawtooth that goes one direction around the quilt, or two directions per side.

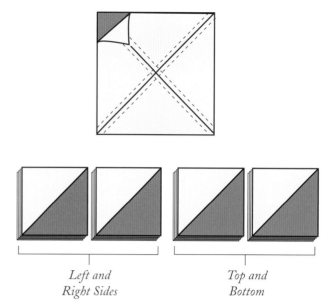

Left and Right Sides　　*Top and Bottom*

Number of Birds Set Straight				
	6" Squares	Total Needed	Left and Right Sides	Top and Bottom
Wallhanging	7	56	14	14
Lap Robe	13	104	32	20
Twin	16	122	38	23
Queen	19	146	41	32
King	22	176	44	44

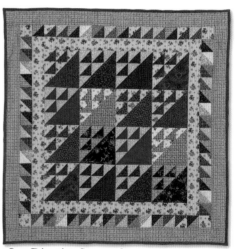

One Direction Sawtooth

Number of Birds on Point				
	6" Squares	Total Needed	Left and Right Sides	Top and Bottom
Wallhanging	7	56	14	14
Lap Robe	14	110	32	23
Twin	16	126	40	23
Queen	20	154	45	32
King	23	180	45	45

Two Direction Sawtooth

One Direction Sawtooth

1. **Take a stack for one side.** Divide Birds into two equal (or nearly equal) stacks.

2. Turn stacks as shown.

3. Flip right sides together, and assembly-line sew stacks.

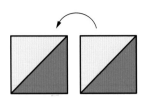

Two stacks for one side

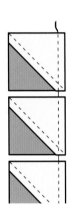

4. Make two stacks of pairs. Flip right sides together, and sew.

5. Repeat until Birds are one strip.

6. Repeat with remaining stacks of Birds until you have a strip for each side.

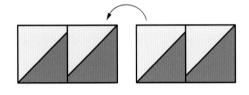

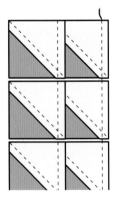

7. Press from wrong side, pressing seams to one side. Press on right side.

8. Skip to Sewing Sawtooth to First Border, page 64.

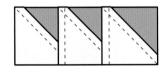

Two Directions Sawtooth

1. **Take a stack for one side.** Divide Birds into four equal stacks. You may have extras.

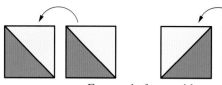

Four stacks for one side

2. Turn stacks as shown. Assembly-line sew.

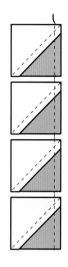
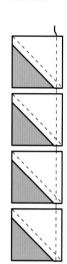

3. Assembly-line sew pairs until you have one strip of Birds for each direction. Press seams to one side.

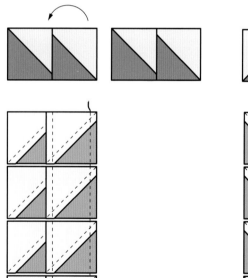

4. Sew directional strips together. Add any extras evenly. A strip longer by one Bird will be hard to detect in a large finished quilt.

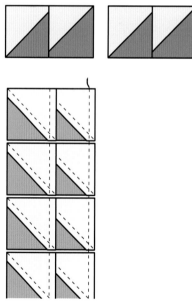

5. Repeat with remaining stacks of Birds until you have a two directional strip for each side.

6. Press seams to left from wrong side. Press on right side.

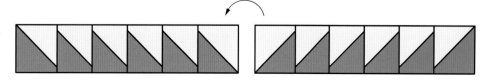

Sewing Sawtooth to First Border

1. Lay Sawtooth strips around quilt.

2. Measure Sawtooth against sides, top, and bottom. If Sawtooth is not same size as First Border, make adjustments.

Longer Sawtooth: Take deeper seams on several until Sawtooth measures the same.

Shorter Sawtooth: Sliver trim First Border until Sawtooth fits.

3. Pin side Sawtooth strips to First Border. If necessary, adjust a few seams to make strip fit. Sew.

4. Press seams away from Sawtooth and toward First Border.

5. Sew 2½" Background squares to the ends of the top and bottom strips. Press seams toward 2½" Background squares.

6. Pin top and bottom strips to First Border and sew.

7. Press seams away from Sawtooth.

8. Add remaining Borders.

Lap Robe Straight Set One Direction

Lap Robe On Point One Direction

Finishing Your Quilt

Layering the Quilt

1. Spread out Backing on a large table or floor area, right side down. Clamp fabric to edge of table with quilt clips, or tape Backing to the floor. Do not stretch Backing.

2. Layer the Batting on the Backing and pat flat.

3. With quilt right side up, center on the Backing. Smooth until all layers are flat. Clamp or tape outside edges.

Safety Pinning

1. Use 1" safety pins with pin covers. Safety pin through all layers in the Nest and in the middle of the Birds. Pin in the Borders every three to five inches, staggering pins so they aren't across from each other.

2. Catch tip of pin in grooves on pinning tool, and close pins.

3. Use pinning tool to open pins when removing them after machine quilting. Store pins opened.

"Stitch in the Ditch" between Blocks and Borders

1. Thread machine with matching thread or invisible thread. If you use invisible thread, loosen top tension. Match the bobbin thread to the Backing.

2. Attach walking foot, and lengthen stitch to 8 to 10 stitches per inch or 3.5 on computerized machines.

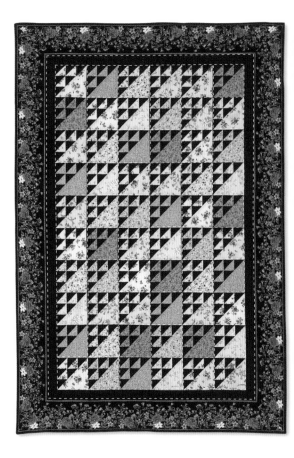

Machine Quilting, set straight

1. Roll the quilt to the middle lengthwise.
   Clip the rolls in place with bicycle clips.

2. Spread the seams open, and "stitch in the ditch" between blocks of vertical rows.

3. Unroll the quilt to the next vertical seam.
   Clip the roll in place, and "stitch in the ditch."
   Repeat until all vertical seams have been quilted.

4. Quilt horizontally until the sides of all blocks have been quilted.

5. "Stitch in the ditch" around the borders.

Machine Quilting, on point

1. Roll the quilt to the middle on the diagonal.
   Clip the rolls in place.

2. Spread the seams open, and "stitch in the ditch" between blocks of the diagonal rows.

3. Unroll the quilt to the next diagonal seam.
   Clip the roll in place, and "stitch in the ditch."
   Repeat until all diagonal seams have been quilted.

4. Quilt all rows on the other diagonal until the 0sides of all blocks have been quilted.

5. "Stitch in the ditch" horizontally through the blocks, avoiding the edge triangles.

6. "Stitch in the ditch" around the borders.

Binding

Use a walking foot attachment and regular thread on top and in the bobbin to match the Binding.

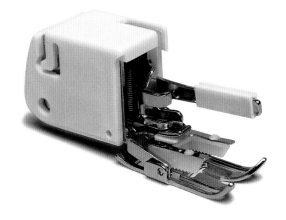

1. Square off the selvage edges, and sew 3" Binding strips together lengthwise.

2. Fold and press in half with wrong sides together.

3. Line up the raw edges of the folded Binding with the raw edges of the quilt in the middle of one side.

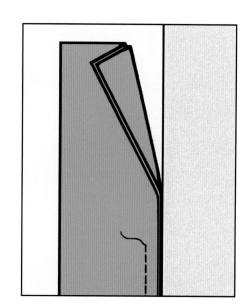

4. Begin stitching 4" from the end of the Binding. Sew with 10 stitches per inch, or 3.0 to 3.5 stitch length on computerized machines. Sew ⅜" from edge, or width of walking foot.

5. At the corner, stop the stitching ⅜" from the edge with the needle in the fabric. Raise the presser foot and turn the quilt to the next side. Put the foot back down.

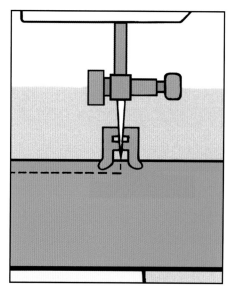

6. Stitch backwards ¼" to the edge of the Binding, raise the foot, and pull the quilt forward slightly.

7. Fold the Binding strip straight up on the diagonal. Fingerpress the diagonal fold.

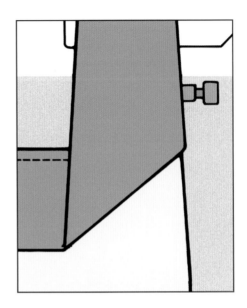

8. Fold the Binding strip straight down with the diagonal fold underneath. Line up the top of the fold with the raw edge of the Binding underneath.

9. Begin sewing from the edge.

10. Continue stitching and mitering the corners around the outside of the quilt.

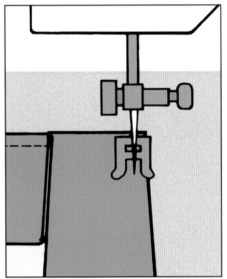

11. Stop stitching 4" from where the ends will overlap.

12. Line up the two ends of Binding. Trim the excess with a ½" overlap.

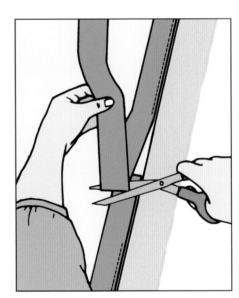

13. Open out the folded ends and pin right sides together. Sew a ¼" seam.

14. Continue to stitch the Binding in place.

15. Trim the Batting and Backing up to the raw edges of the Binding.

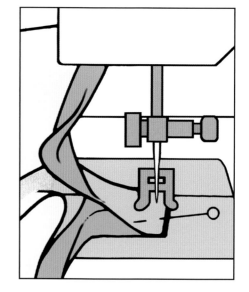

16. Fold the Binding to the back side of the quilt. Pin in place so that the folded edge on the Binding covers the stitching line. Tuck in the excess fabric at each miter on the diagonal.

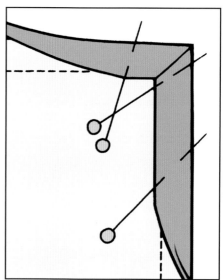

17. From the right side, "stitch in the ditch" using invisible thread on the front side, and a bobbin thread to match the Binding on the back side. Catch the folded edge of the Binding on the back side with the stitching.

Optional: Hand stitch Binding in place.

18. Sew an identification label on the Back.

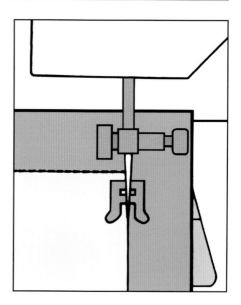

A grateful thank you to all the quiltmakers.

Sue Bouchard
Lori Forsythe
Patricia Knoechel
Lyn Sethna
Loretta Smith
Lois Thornhill
Teresa Varnes

Index

Order Information

Quilt in a Day books offer a wide range of techniques and are directed toward a variety of skill levels.
If you do not have a quilt shop in your area, you may write or call for a complete catalog and current
price list of all books and patterns published by Quilt in a Day®, Inc.

Quilt in a Day®, Inc. • 1955 Diamond Street • San Marcos, CA 92069
1 800 777-4852 • Fax: (760) 591-4424 • www.quiltinaday.com

Peacocks of a Feather Flock Together

Lyn Sethna's bright quilt is worth strutting about! She gathered 15 different jazzy fabrics, and made four blocks from each one. Side triangles cut from 10½" squares of the same intense fabrics encase and settle the vibrant blocks set on point.

French Connection

Sue Bouchard dug into her treasured bag of fabrics from Provence, France for this colorful rendition of Birds in the Air. For a festive look, Sue mixed the Birds and Nests, and added multiple colors of Side Triangles cut from 5¼" x 11" pieces. See page 52 for cutting instructions. A 2½" Simple Border, an American fabric from Doreen Speckman's line, frames this charming quilt.

Blue Birds of Happiness

Lois Thornhill selected a flock of blue fabrics in varying scales of prints for her straight set blocks. Several Birds with red feathers flew in for the excitement. She created her own Border with left-over pairs of Birds sewn into flying geese patches. A 2½" Background strip and block corners set this lovely quilt in flight.

Cardinals Always Come in Pairs

Lyn Sethna chose rich brown tones for Nests filled with contented Bluejays. For excitement she added Cardinals to two of the Nests, plus a tiny appliqued Lady Bug for good luck! See page 33 for how to strategically place the red birds. Lyn machine quilted ¼" from Nest and Side Triangle seams, and flew around the Birds with stippling. This beautiful quilt is something to squawk about!